# *Pinterest*

## TRAFFIC SECRETS

## How To Get Traffic From The Fastest Growing Social Site Online!

Leather Sandals with Ankle Strap in Blue

Pinned by
Earmack Social Bridgette S.B.

The Covered Foot

Sleeveless Blouse in

rk Social Bridgette S.B.

ng and Style

Mediterranean Chicken L
Wrap Tacos (Only 350 cal

62 repins  12 likes

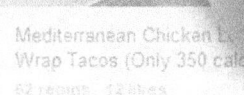
aimee * artsyville

Guest-Pinner: Aimee of Arts...

Dark Cho

Ear

Fee

Flamenc

3 Piece Classics Nesting Table Set

PINTEREST
Traffic Secrets

By E.W. Bailor

# Table of Contents

## Introduction To Pinterest Traffic Secrets

Social media is the darling of the Internet. For the past few years, online user activity has been shifting more and more toward social media of all types, but recently it has truly become an almost entirely visual format. Gone are the days where text-based communications dominated the social scene. These days, it's all about visual stimulation and contact through engaging pictures and videos.

No website has made this more evident than Pinterest. Pinterest allows users to share photos and other media by "pinning" them to virtual pin boards. Remember the former popularity of corkboards? Pinterest has brought that concept online in a big way!

According to Alexa.com, Pinterest is currently 15$^{th}$ in the United States and 34$^{th}$ in the world for traffic volume. The site gets a tremendous amount of traffic, and those users are known to visit the site regularly **and** to purchase products and visit websites they see there.

In fact, MediaBistro.com compiled a report about social networking tools and discovered that almost as many people use Pinterest as use Twitter!

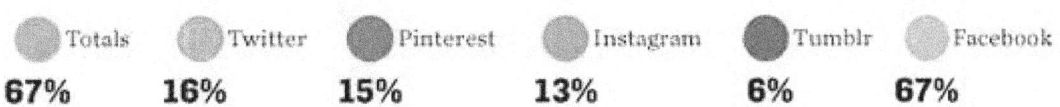

| Totals | Twitter | Pinterest | Instagram | Tumblr | Facebook |
|--------|---------|-----------|-----------|--------|----------|
| **67%** | **16%** | **15%** | **13%** | **6%** | **67%** |

In this guide, you're going to learn how to make the most of this social media powerhouse, and how to use it **effectively** as a marketing tool.

*So let's get started.*

## Quick & Easy Setup

New websites are confusing and time-consuming for anyone. Even the most tech savvy user always has a learning curve when using a site for the first time. Unless you've been using Pinterest for a while, you'll need a little help getting started. Even if you have been using Pinterest for a while, there are probably features you haven't used or don't know about that could really boost your efforts considerably!

Before you get started, take a moment to familiarize yourself with the Pinterest interface so you will know where you need to go in order to perform the basic functions associated with managing your Pinterest account.

First, take a look at the menu that drops down when you hover over your name at the top right of the Pinterest website:

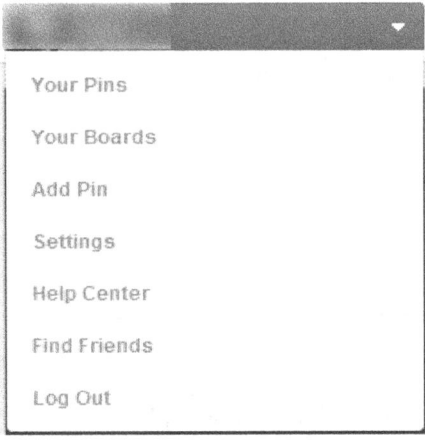

As you can see, this menu contains several options:

- Your Pins – This takes you to a page that shows you everything you have already pinned. It will also allow you to add a new pin.

- Your Boards – This takes you to a page that shows you all of the boards you have created. It will also allow you to create a new board.
- Add Pin – This will pop up a window that allows you to upload a new pin from your computer.
- Settings – Be sure to familiarize yourself with this page, because this is where you will set up your profile!
- Help Center – If you have questions or need help, see this page.
- Find Friends – This will help you find other Pinterest users to connect with.
- Log Out – Log out of your Pinterest account.

## Creating an Optimized Profile

The first thing you need to do to get started on Pinterest is create your profile page. This page is a place for you to really grab users and get them interested. This page should contain the very best of your pins, as well as important information about yourself and your business.

If you have a Facebook account, you can connect your Pinterest account to it for an additional boost. The catch? You can't connect your Pinterest account to a business page, only a personal Facebook profile.

You can also connect your Pinterest account to your Twitter account. When you do this, your pins will automatically be shared on your Twitter account. This is useful even if you don't have many followers on Twitter.

This automatic sharing on Twitter and Facebook is a huge part of what made Pinterest such an overnight success. About 75% of Pinterest users choose to integrate at least one other social platform, which greatly increases the number of people who see their pins.

## The About Section

The "About" section is another important part of your profile. It should contain a paragraph or two about you and your company, making sure to include vital information such as your website or blog URLs and some keywords for search engines.

## Adding Value to your Profile

One of the most important things you can do to increase the power of your Pinterest profile is to use a headshot image of yourself instead of a logo or other image. If you don't like the way you look, or you're using a pseudonym, you can find a very realistic looking stock photo or use a picture of one very close-up feature of yourself such as an eye or your lips. Just make it very personal.

Do not forget to include your important URLs on your profile, such as your blog or website, Facebook profile URL, Twitter profile URL and other relevant URLs.

# Social Connect

It cannot be expressed enough the importance of connecting your Pinterest account to a Facebook account and to a Twitter account and allowing Pinterest to automatically post to those sites.

It will significantly improve your efforts if you take the time to do this, because you are likely to have a larger number of followers on Facebook or Twitter than you do on the Pinterest site itself, and this will get your content more views.

In order to connect your Pinterest account to your Facebook and/or Twitter account, simply visit your Settings page and use the sliders to turn on logging into Facebook and Twitter and publishing activity to your Facebook Timeline. Then click the "Save Profile" button.

## Pinning Content

There are three main ways to pin content to your boards:

1. You can upload an image from your computer.
2. You can use the "Pin it" button.
3. You can re-pin content other people have pinned.

Each of these methods has its uses, and we'll talk about those now.

Uploading an Image or Pinning from a URL

In order to upload an image from your computer, you can click the "Add Pin" link from the dropdown box at the top right. This will bring up a menu that looks like this:

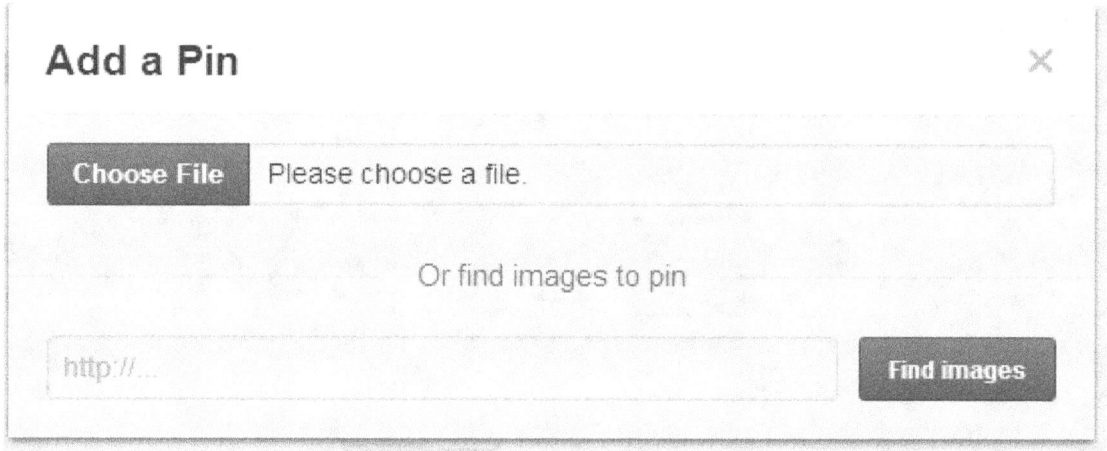

To upload from your hard drive, click "Choose File" and select the image. To find an image on a web page, enter the page's URL and click "Find images".

Here is the result of entering a URL:

Images from http://8images.wordpress.com/

Each of these images can be pinned by simply hovering over the image and clicking the "Pin it" button.

## Pinning with a Browser Add-On

You can also pin content directly using a browser add-on. For example, Chrome has an extension that will let you pin content by putting a "Pin It" button in your bookmarks bar at the top of the page under the URL window.

If you install the add-on, all you have to do is visit any web page, click the "Pin It" button in your bookmarks bar, and it will give you a choice of images you can then pin.

Here is an example:

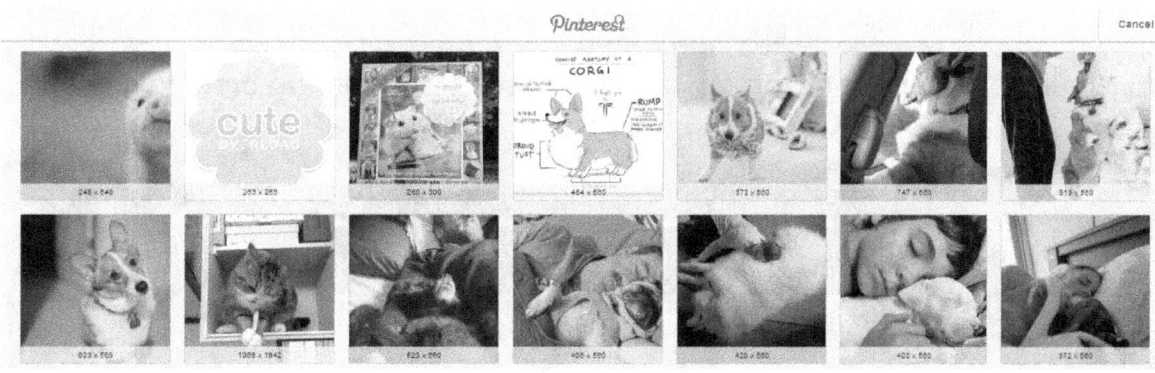

Whenever you find something you would like to share that someone else has posted on Pinterest, just click the "Pin it" button to re-pin it to your own board. Just look for the button that appears when you hover over an image or when you click the image the button appears at the top left.

Pinning Tips

Here are some important things to keep in mind as you pin items:

1. Activity on Pinterest peaks around 5-7 AM and again from 5-7 PM Eastern time. Plan most of your pinning for those time periods in order to maximize how many people view your content.

2. Try to pin unique content that is relevant to your business. You can also pin funny or interesting items that will grab attention, but keep most of your pins focused on your area of marketing.

3. Be sure to include keywords in all of your pin and board descriptions to attract search engine traffic.
4. Choose the most attractive images possible. If there are several different shots of the same item, choose the one that is most visually appealing, as people are naturally drawn to aesthetically pleasing images.
5. Focus on lifestyle, not products. Don't just show a package of potato chips. Show a family eating potato chips at a family picnic.

# Engage For Maximum Traffic

There are many ways to fully engage your audience in order to make your efforts more effective. By engaging your Pinterest followers with direct contact from you, they will see you more as an individual rather than a company, which will increase your trust level considerably.

We're going to take a look at some of the ways you can engage your audience to boost your traffic and sales.

## Contests

There are many types of contests you can hold to increase loyalty and also gain more followers in the process. For example, you can hold a contest for the most referrals, the most re-pins of your content, one random person who re-pins one of your pins, give additional entries to people who also post your pins on Facebook and Twitter, etc.

Get creative with your contests. And remember, the ultimate goal is to get your pins seen by more people and to gain more followers. So focus your contest rules on getting people to help you achieve that.

## Commenting on your Own Pins

Interaction is important, especially on highly social sites like Pinterest. When people comment on your pins, be sure to communicate back. Keep an open line of dialog with your followers. Once they see you as a real person, they'll begin to like you as a person and will re-pin your content more often and respond better to the things you pin.

### Cross Promoting on Facebook and Twitter

Even if you don't want to hook your Pinterest account directly up to your Facebook or Twitter account and have your pins shared automatically, you can still take advantage of these sites to cross-promote.

Just be sure you share your most important pins to your Facebook, Twitter, and other social media accounts for maximum exposure.

### Follow Relevant Users

Another great way to get more views of your pins as well as more followers is to follow other people who post content similar to yours. Don't worry about the "competition" factor. There's plenty of room for everyone.

Let's say you are in the golf niche. Follow other people who are avid golfers and have a significant number of followers. Not only might they re-pin your content, especially if they see you re-pin theirs sometimes, but you can comment on their pins and potentially get more followers that way as well.

### Post Pins to Blogs, Forums, Newsletters, Etc.

Make sure to post links to your most important pins to places like relevant blogs (in the comments and on your own blog), relevant forums, email newsletters, as your email signature, and other locations.

### Use Video for More Exposure

Video sites like YouTube are extremely effective traffic sources, and they can easily help you get more views to your pins. Simply post a video relevant to your pin and link to your pin in the description of your video.

Not only that, but you could post a link to your pin in the comments of other relevant videos that have a significant number of views. This way, you can get some traffic from other people as well. Just be sure your pin is useful and relevant or it will be seen as spam.

## Ask for Re-pins on Important Pins

Sales people have heard the old adage, "To **get** the sale, you have to **ask** for the sale." The same goes for re-pins. Sure, you'll get the occasional re-pin without asking, but when you post something really important, just ask people to re-pin it for you. You'll be surprised how many people will oblige, especially if you've engaged them prior to asking and they like you.

Just remember not to abuse the privilege. If you ask people to re-pin every post, people will eventually get tired of it and won't do it anymore. Save this technique for your most important pins and for those with the most potential to go viral.

## Re-pin For Others

Don't forget to re-pin content for your followers. If they see you re-pinning their content, they will be much more likely to reciprocate and pin yours. Additionally, they may even feel obligated to do so, because they've seen you re-pin theirs.

## Pinterest Tools

While you can certainly use Pinterest without any additional tools, there are a few things you might want to consider that will make using Pinterest easier and more effective.

## Graphics Programs

One thing you will almost certainly want to have if you're going to use Pinterest regularly is a good image editing program. You can download a few trial of Adobe Photoshop, but the software is very expensive to buy beyond the trial. However, if you like it, you can use Adobe Creative Cloud to access Photoshop and other software for a lower monthly fee instead of having to pay for it upfront and spending hundreds of dollars at once.

If you'd rather not spend any money at all, you can try GIMP, which stands for GNU Image Manipulation Program. This software isn't quite as full-featured as Photoshop, nor does it have as many free add-ons available, but it is free and works very well.

>> http://www.adobe.com/products/creativecloud.html
>> http://www.gimp.org

## Pinpuff

Pinpuff is a service that will give you some simple analytics about your Pinterest account, such as an approximate value of each pin, your potential CPC, your reach score (how many followers you have compared to others), your virality score (how well people re-pin your content) and other data.

This can be especially useful for determining the effectiveness of your Pinterest campaigns, allowing you to make changes, if needed.

>> http://www.pinpuff.com

## PinReach

PinReach is quite similar to Pinpuff, except it offers a lot more data. You'll find pages for general analytics, as well as an analysis of your boards, a collection of your post popular pins, your most influential followers (great for finding out who has the most potential to re-pin your content to great effect), and more!

>> http://www.pinreach.com

## Pinterest Right-Click for Firefox

If you have the Firefox web browser, you can get an extension that will add an additional menu item to your right-click menu. That way, if you run across an interesting image online, you can simply right click it and immediately select "Pin Image" to pin the image without having to visit Pinterest first.

>> https://addons.mozilla.org/en-US/firefox/addon/pinterest-right-click/

Pinterest Pro for Chrome

If you use Chrome, you can download the Pinterest Pro extension that will give you the right-click feature available in Pinterest Right-Click for Firefox, plus also gives you image zooming and a "Popular Pin Dropdown". Once installed, it works the same way as Pinterest Right-Click. Just right click and image and click "Pin to Pinterest."

\>\>
https://chrome.google.com/webstore/detail/nfbooeikickobcebioomphnekojoelip

Pin Search for Chrome

Another useful Chrome extension is Pin Search. This will let you quickly find more information about any photo you find on Pinterest. Simply install it and the whenever you hover over a pinned image using Chrome, you'll see a new button that says "Search". Click this and it will open Google's search results page that will show you similar images, other sizes of that image online, and l inks where you might be able to find more information.

\>\>https://chrome.google.com/webstore/detail/okiaciimfpgbpdhnfdllhdkicpmdoakm

## Final Words

If you're not using Pinterest for marketing, you are missing out on some of the best quality traffic available anywhere online. Pinterest users are famous for their clicking and their buying, which makes it more than just another traffic source. In fact, Shopify.com reports that visitors referred from Pinterest are at least 10% more likely to buy and generally spend at least 10% more than people who are referred from other social sites, and 70% more than people referred from a website! The average order from someone referred from Pinterest is double those referred from Facebook, and even more than Google, Amazon and other search engines. So don't miss out! Start using Pinterest today!

## Resources

Learn how to get an unbelievable amount of traffic, get more sales, boost your opt-ins, outrank nearly any website and much more with Video Profits Fastlane!

>> http://videoprofitsfastlane.com/

Pinterest has absolutely exploded in the short time since its inception, and people are using it to drive massive amounts of extremely high-quality traffic! Find out how you can jump on this bandwagon with Pinterest Fastlane!

>> http://www.pinterestfastlane.com/

Discover the fastest, easiest squeeze funnel builder and optimizer and learn how you can capture more leads faster than ever before!

>> http://squeezeninja.com/

Bring your marketing into the 21st century using these explosively powerful social marketing techniques!

>> http://empoweria.com/wp/socialpowersecrets/

I wish you much success

Cancel

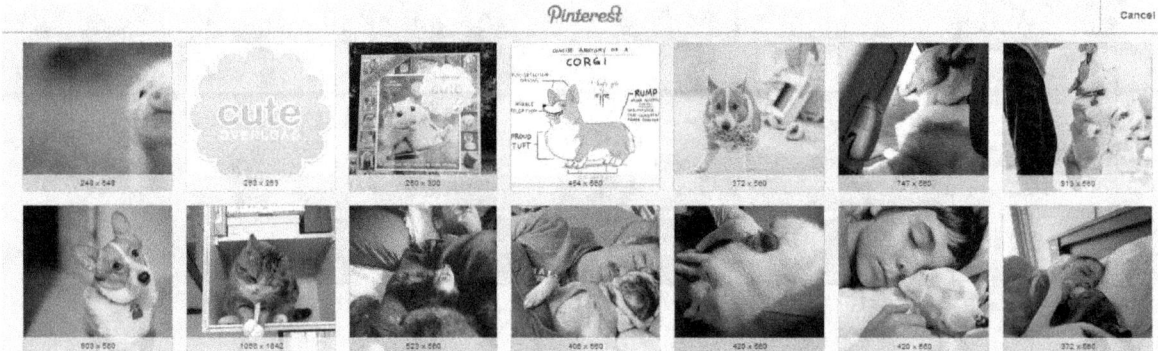

For Kirsten

This page intentionally left blank

Thank you